From a New Forest Inclosure

Book Five 2012 & 2013

By

Ian Thew

Published by Burley Rails Publishing
Burley Rails Cottage BH24 4HT
Printed by DPI Dorset

ISBN 978-0-9570835-4-7

Ian Thew

Born in Southampton, Ian and his siblings were brought, throughout their childhood, into the New Forest to walk and enjoy the open space. Although, initially, he spent his adult life living and working away from  the Forest he was always keen on the countryside and country sports, especially fishing and shooting. He returned whenever he could to the Forest until, eventually, he settled down in Burley with his late wife, Diane. In 1994 they moved to the remote Burley Rails Cottage which, originally built as a woodman's cottage and sold by the Forestry Commission in the 1960's, is a unique place in which to live.

Ian's knowledge of the forest is genuine and he is respected for his considerate and well researched articles which are published in national and international magazines.

These booklets have been produced with the encouragement of readers who wished to refer to a particular article which had been lost in a discarded magazine and at the suggestion of those who wanted friends, relatives and visitors in general to understand the Forest and its ways. So whether a Villager, Visitor, Tourist, or Grockle, whatever your guise, we hope these snippets will help you to understand what is so very special about this wonderful place.

Following the success of the previous collections of articles written, originally, for the Burley Village magazine, 'From a New Forest Inclosure Book Five' is a compilation of the articles published in 2012 and 2013 which have been enhanced by the authors' own colour photographs.

Within these pages you will find amusing tales about Bill. Read about my family and on-going life in the inclosure.

Ian Thew

January

I'm pleased to say that the Doting Owner of the Spoilt Pony is a very good cook who panders to the needs of all the members of this ménage. This pampered existence has its downside, however, and it's fair to note that one or two of the household were, to say the least, gaining weight and when I say gaining weight, perhaps I should be saying they were downright fat! Some of you will know that my own figure is not as trim as it should be but who am I to refuse this surfeit of delicious calories which keep my naturally, sylph-like figure, hidden from view!! But it wasn't me that I was concerned for, it was the dogs, of course, and in deference to their well-being, their daily intake of nutrients has, for some time now, been restricted by the introduction of a sensible, canine diet. Gone, are the titbits, the left-over's and the doggie chocs and instead a single, suitably designed meal followed by a dog biscuit at bed time constitutes their daily intake of food. And are they happy with this rather harsh regime – no, of course they're not! But, nonetheless, the excess weight began to fall-off and waistlines started to reappear-but not for long. Gradually, despite their continued dietary routine, the pesky pooches, once again, piled-on the pounds and we wondered how this could possibly be.

We were soon to discover that our canine companions had turned into enterprising and sometimes furtive thieves. The first evidence was encountered, one evening, when we discovered the larder door open and the contents of three large bags of baking flour distributed across the kitchen floor. The culprits, three flour-coated dogs, looked up, from this scene of destruction, with snowy muzzles and little sign of remorse. We were, of course, dismayed by our discovery but, after evicting the offending hounds, we began to see the funny side of the incident until, that is, we came to clear up the mess. The vacuum cleaner coped with the bulk of the powder but it was only when we tried to mop-up the residue that I was reminded of my Father who, years ago, mixed flour and water for use as a wallpaper paste! I'm sure that by now you've got the gist of where this is heading so I'll leave the rest to your imagination but suffice it to say that scrubbing brushes and strong language came into the remedial equation!!

A few days later we were to discover another illicit food source and at the same time solve a niggling mystery. The Doting Owner of the Spoilt Pony keeps chickens and as a supplement to their regular diet of pellets she mashes any stale bread, pastry etc. and feeds it to them in their run. She had remarked, in passing, that despite licking the bowl clean on a daily basis the hens looked rather skinny and why, she asked, did they always lay their eggs in the higher nesting boxes and never in the lower ones. I was unable to enlighten her, at the time, but it was not long before the truth was out.

Flour-covered, kitchen floor

Soon after, I noticed, through the window, my cocker spaniel crossing the lawn in a determined fashion. She was heading for the chicken run. She looked over her shoulder, as she neared it, to see if she was being observed and, satisfied that she was in the clear, she jumped up and through the pop-hole into the hen house. Without hesitation she jumped through the other pop-hole down into the wire run where she greedily devoured the chickens' mash. To add insult to injury I discovered, when I went to reprimand her, that on her exit from the run she had helped herself to an egg from one of the lower nesting boxes!!

Don't get too eggcited and have a very happy New Year

February

'It's an ill wind that blows nobody any good' is an idiom that has been knocking around in the English language in one form or another since the mid fifteen hundreds. This adage crossed my mind recently as I lay in bed in the early hours of the morning listening to a hooligan of a wind that was screaming through the Forest trees and moaning about the house. Doors rattled and windows shook and every so often the ghostly and spine-chilling voice of the wind haunted the eaves. Downstairs the dogs barked and, during an occasional lull between the violent gusts, the steel shoes of the spoilt pony could be heard on the stable yard as she grew more and more restless with this exceptional storm.

The dark, early hours of the morning are renowned as the most depressing time of day and my mind began to imagine the most horrible repercussions; will the big oak tree that towers over the front of the house come crashing down?; will the stable roof be there in the morning?; will the fences remain intact and will we lose our electricity supply? My gloomy contemplations were dashed into insignificance by the sudden, painful crack of a splitting, submitting limb followed by the house-shaking thump as it crashed to the ground. I'd like to say that I bravely donned my gear and went out into the tempest to investigate – but I can't. I drew the duvet tight around me and tried hard to dispel from my thoughts the enumerable disasters that might be happening outside.

After a couple more hours without sleep, dawn began to reveal the mayhem outside. Through the window, the trees were in turmoil; thrashing into each other with such ferocity that it seemed that the whole Forest would come crashing down at any minute. A daylight inspection revealed two fallen and substantial beech limbs, fortunately, just beyond the perimeter fence and a section of stock fencing that had been broken by a frightened pony that was temporarily lodged in the bottom paddock. Our property, thank goodness, had survived the ordeal with a minimum of damage; the not-so-ill wind subsided and the sun showed and all seemed well with our part of the world.

There's another old adage, however, something about not counting chickens until they're hatched! During that night the wind returned with a vengeance and once more sleep was lost because of the sheer noise and ferocity of the storm The next morning the lights flickered a few times and then finally died and all power to the property died with them. Although inconvenient, I was not too disturbed by this turn of events - after all there was, sitting in the workshop, a recently overhauled and serviced generator – wasn't there?

I removed the cover from the 'genny' pulled and pushed all the appropriate knobs and turned the key. My efforts were rewarded with a feeble groan from the starting motor – the battery was as dead as a Dodo. Fortunately the machine is equipped, for just such a situation, with a pull cord and after much pulling, sweating and not a little swearing the engine burst into life and settled down to a reassuring tick-over, as it should do. I was pleased with my success and decided that, now we had some power, a hot cup of tea would be the first item on the agenda - not so, I'm afraid. After a few minutes the engine revs increased dramatically and thick smoke appeared from somewhere below and the production of home-brewed electricity came to an abrupt halt!

Victim of a storm

Fortunately, the good engineers from the Electricity Board restored our supply by late afternoon and I did, after all, manage to purchase the fallen limbs which will keep us warm next winter, so perhaps it is an ill wind that blows nobody any good.

Must go now – I'm getting puffed-out!

March

We weren't here the day that Charlie Fox came to pay us a visit. In fact we were far away across the Forest and out of mobile phone signal. He came, no doubt, to inspect our free-range chickens that enjoy their existence in and around the cottage garden; safe in the knowledge that there are three, free-range dogs on the premises to look out for them.

I don't know what happened to the guard dogs on the day in question. I do recall that the spaniel was with us all day, leaving the geriatric Labrador and Jack Russell 'on duty'; and their poor hearing, which, like mine, has deteriorated with age and abuse, may account for their total ignorance of the events that I'm about to relate.

Enjoying the ball after rounding up the chickens

It was late afternoon and my step-daughter, who was home from university in order to attend a ball that very evening, had just taken a bath. She was making some final adjustments to her appearance, as only girlies do, when she happened to glance out of the window and there, to her shock horror, walking boldly across the lawn, with a chicken clamped firmly in its jaws, was a large fox!!

She immediately opened the bathroom window and shouted and hollered for all she was worth and Charlie, true to form, dived for cover in a nearby clump of Rhododendrons. A few seconds later, and much to her relief, she spotted the raiding Reynard skulking away across the Forest floor, without the aforementioned hen which soon appeared, none the worse for its encounter, from the depths of the shrubbery.

Confident that she had out-foxed the offending fox, the young lady returned to her pre-ball preparations. Not five minutes later, she happened to glance through the window and was alarmed to see the persistent Charlie creeping back towards the garden. Now this time she was really angry and, without further ado, she hastily donned a white robe and charged down the stairs and into the garden. Screaming for all she was worth and scattering chickens as she went, she tore across the lawn and drove the fox back into the Forest, from whence it came. Now what she didn't realise is that our land is very wet in Winter and, consequently, she came to a standstill, in what is probably best described as a mire, minus footwear and with thick mud splattered up her legs and over her once white robe; and, to add to her troubles, she was due to leave the house, ready for the ball, in less than an hour.

She tried to phone us for advice and, of course, got no reply. She phoned her boy friend, a wise Forest lad, who told her to be sure and lock the chickens in the hen house before she left for the ball and not to be late, either! In desperation, she grabbed the first things that came to hand – a fish slice and a wooden spoon!! – and sallied forth, once more, to drive the chickens into their run.

Now our chickens are creatures of habit. They're used to putting themselves to bed when they are good and ready. They don't like being pushed around and can become extremely stubborn when under duress. My step-daughter told me, after the event, just how difficult a task it had been and I conjured-up a picture of this pretty, determined, barefoot, muddy, young lady, crouched with arms outstretched, a fish slice in one hand and a wooden spoon in the other as she tried to drive our hens to safety.

But like any genuine, Forest girl, drive them in, she did; and with the birds safely locked away from Charlie, she did go to the ball where, I'm sure, she turned many a young man's head!

Must go now, before I get the brush-off

April

If I were to tell you that my old Wellington boots are desirable you'll think that I am stark, staring mad! Some of the less charitable of you might assume that I'd overstayed my welcome at the pub or, worse still, had been surreptitiously sipping the amber liquid! Well, you'd be wrong on both counts and I can tell you, quite categorically, that sometimes my waterproof footwear seems to be not only irresistible but downright desirable. Now, don't get me wrong, as far as I'm concerned, boots are boots - just essential accoutrements to anyone who, like me, has elected to live in the heart of the Forest. Why then should others find them so

Lucky toads on the door mat

appealing? A strange question, you might think, but, recently, we've experienced some odd occurrences, up here in the Inclosure, and on each occasion my boots have been the epicentre of attention. Let me tell you more!

Boots, as I've already said, are indispensable for our way of life and you'll find them around every doorway into our cottage. Green Wellies, black

Wellies, riding boots, walking boots, and even work boots – you name them and they'll be there. Some standing neatly in pairs and others scattered over the doorstep where they have been discarded in a hurry or knocked flat by over ebullient pooches. Now, not so long ago, when I was in a bit of a rush, I hastily righted a fallen boot and promptly shoved my stocking-clad foot into it – immediately I knew something was wrong. I felt something soft and yielding and quickly withdrew the aforementioned appendage. The boot was upturned and shaken and out fell a toad – yes, a toad, and a very dead toad at that. Unfortunately, my size nine 'hoofer' was too much for the tiny amphibian and I'm sad to say that I'd inadvertently killed it.

The very next morning, I had occasion to repeat the process and this time I slipped, rather than shoved, my foot into a Wellie and thank goodness that I'd erred on the side of caution for, sure enough, there again, inside my Wellie I felt something squidgy – but, this time, it was not one, but two toads, that fell onto the doormat when I emptied the boot!! And, I'm pleased to say, they both crawled away, none the worse for the experience.

But it didn't end there. Oh no! Just recently I found, laid across the threshold, what I supposed was a dead mouse. The cat that was nearby, watching; and assuming that the deceased rodent was his doing I went to find something with which to remove it. When I returned the mouse had gone - disappeared, vanished, scarpered - or whatever mice do. Then I spotted the cat that was sniffing around – you've guessed it – one of my Wellies! And, sure enough, when the boot was shaken, out dropped a mouse – a dead mouse! It must have been 'playing possum' to fool the cat and had, somehow, managed to hide in my footwear. Now think on this. The mouse had to be alive when it sought refuge in my boot but why then did it make that final journey to the 'Big Cheeseboard in the Sky'? I wonder what could be so fatal about the inside of my Wellies?

On a footwear related note, I heard a tale of a local lad of six years of age who, just recently, was on the Forest with his Granddad looking for animal tracks. In a particularly muddy spot, they came upon the imprint of a stout walking boot.

"What's that?" asked the grandparent, pointing at the impression.

"A Townies' footprint." was the unerring and unexpected reply.

"But how do you know it's a Townies?" asked the surprised man

"That's easy, only a Townie would walk in the mud. A Forester would have the sense to walk around it!!"

Must go now, before I too am defeeted!

May

I thought I'd got the better of the weeds, this year, in the kitchen garden. The long, dry spell that we experienced, prior to Easter, had kept them at bay and I was almost convinced that my extensive activity, last season, with the hoe was proving to be worthwhile. But, alas, how wrong could I be, a few sprinklings of rain and the previously bare soil is, once again, a carpet of fresh, green seedlings. Oh well, it'll be out with the hoe again!

Seriously though, that unusually warm weather, which had resulted in hose pipe restrictions in our neighbouring counties, was the cause for some concern; and how pleasant it was, after a day of heavy rain, to walk out through Mouses Cupboard and up through Soarley Beeches to return via Stinking Edge Wood and Gods' Gate. The thorough soaking had worked wonders. In the Inclosure the oak trees were starting to dress themselves for the summer and, alongside the path on the open Forest, blue-eyed violets peeped out from among the tangle of new-sprung whortleberry and the dead, bracken stalks of last autumn. The willows and silver birches flaunted their flowering catkins and, all around, the myriad of bird song was welcomed by these ageing ears.

The Easter holiday brought the usual influx of visitors to this most beautiful part of England. Most of those, who ventured this far into the Forest, seemed to be enjoying the unique experience of being able to walk or cycle through our tracks and by-ways – but not all. In fact some visitors are just about as welcome, in this Forest of ours, as brass knobs on wooden fence posts!

Whilst busily baking, one morning during the holiday, the doting owner of the spoilt pony was disturbed from her thoughts by sudden and incessant barking from the dogs. Thinking that they were just announcing the presence of a passer-by, she ordered them to be quiet and continued with her bread making. When, after about a minute or so, they had not taken her advice, she left her floury dough and went to investigate the cause of their concern.

She opened the gate and, accompanied by the nosey cat, walked onto the Forest track. There was nothing there! The dogs, meanwhile, were still barking wildly at the side fence and when she peered around the corner she spotted two young boys who, giggling madly, were pushing their bicycles against the fence in order to enrage the dogs.

"What do you think you are doing?" she yelled.

The boys jumped with shock and surprise and turned in unison to face the most unexpected apparition.

"N,n,nothing." stuttered one of the frightened lads as he eyed this seemingly fearsome and furious woman whose long, greying locks were somewhat awry, and around whose flour-dusted pinafore stared a malevolent-eyed, jet-black moggie.

"Where are your parents?" she demanded.

"B,b, back there." A trembling finger pointed to the cross-road. "They told us to ride ahead and out of their way." He added.

"And where are you riding too?" she asked

"B,B,Burley" he stammered.

"Burley is that way" she pointed up the track. "So get going and be quick about it".

The Doting Owner of the Spoilt Pony

She chuckled to herself as they wobbled-off, as fast as their little legs would pedal, up the hill towards the village. She soon regretted, however, her hasty deliverance. Perhaps she should have been more understanding? But, on the other hand, she was certain that, having just caught a glimpse of herself in the mirror, they would be on their best behaviour for the rest of their holiday, in the Forest.

Burley is, after all, renowned for its association with witches!!

Isn't it?

June

Apparently, isolation and insanity, as far as some people are concerned, go hand in hand. How often have we heard ' *You have to be mad to live up here'* and, quite frankly , I like to hear it; I'm pleased that living in the depths of this beautiful Forest is not everyone's 'cup of tea'! But isolation, when you are part of a community such as ours, is not an issue. Removed and remote from the village we might be but excluded we are not; which was borne out by a recent incident. Let me tell you more!

It was Sunday afternoon and I was minding my own business and happily murdering weeds in the kitchen garden when my ancient ears were assailed by some serious shouting – my name was being bandied, at full volume, across the Forest. Something was not right; so I abandoned my tools and went to investigate. It transpired that the daughter of the doting owner of the spoilt pony had feinted; and not only that, her extremities had turned a nasty shade of blue! Without delay, an ambulance was summoned and because satellite navigation doesn't recognise our post code (hurrah) I was despatched to the main road in order to guide it to the house. I had no sooner arrived at the gate when a small, yellow vehicle with a flashing, blue light came hurrying down the road preceded by our very own Tim Gray in his own vehicle. Apparently, the driver of this 'first response vehicle', a specially trained fireman from Ringwood, who had no idea where we were located, had called Tim, who is Watch Manager for our Burley fire crew, for help. The off-duty Tim, without hesitation and in his own inimitable way had said 'follow me', or words to that effect, - and there they were.

Having arrived back at the cottage I was immediately advised by this First Responder that an ambulance was on the Forest, somewhere, trying to locate us; so off I went, once again, in search of said ambulance. I didn't have to go far, for as I arrived at the first crossroads in our access track, I was surprised and pleased to see the aforementioned ambulance, preceded by a private car, approaching from the direction of Anderwood. I did a quick U-turn and the car pulled over and let the ambulance fall-in behind my vehicle. I discovered later that the driver of the car was my 'neighbour', David, from Burley lodge who, having discovered a misplaced ambulance on his doorstep and being a sensible sort of chap, had decided that action rather than words was the order of the day and so, rather than waste a lot of time on complicated directions, he jumped in his car and led the ambulance through the Forest to our house.

Daughter of the Doting Owner of the Spoilt Pony

And it doesn't end there! A few minutes after the ambulance had arrived a Forestry Commission vehicle pulled up on the gravel and out jumped Howard, our local keeper ,who had heard over the 'Forest drums' that something was amiss up in the Inclosure and, without hesitation, he had hurried over to see if he could offer any help.

Fortunately, the young lady had suffered nothing more serious than a particularly nasty 'bug' of some description; and so after cups of tea and biscuits, all round, the cavalcade of vehicles departed and peace reigned over the Inclosure once again. But how fortunate are we to live in this village with such good and caring friends and neighbours? To everyone involved on that day, Tracy, Harriet and I would like to say a big **'THANKYOU'**.

Isolated, remote, cut-off? – You must be joking!

July

The swallows have returned. They're a bit later than usual, but never mind, I always look forward to their safe return. They were first spotted a couple of weeks ago as they darted in and out of the stables wherein they had nested, with mixed success, over recent years; but this time they had arrived to find an interloper in their midst! An enterprising wren has carried-out a quick conversion (without planning permission) on their favoured nest by adding a dome of moss and lichens to their neat, earthy bowl. A similar invasion of their privacy occurred in 2007 at which time the swallows that were in residence, simply tossed-out the offending material, gave the wrens a severe telling-off and proceeded to rear a brood or two before departing to foreign climes, once more.

Swallows nest taken over by wrens

Now, the swallows of today, it seems, lack the backbone of their forebears and having been 'faced-down' by a pair of angry, vociferous wrens these aerial acrobats went in search of a new home – and they found it without having to go far- in my workshop! Smack-bang in the centre and not five feet above my workbench they have built, without a 'by-your-leave' or a 'do you mind', a new nest. A coil of electric cable hanging on a nail has provided the footings and from here they have constructed in a few days, from mud, horsehair and goodness knows what else, a most remarkable feat of engineering.

I'm busy with a project, at the moment, that requires the use of the aforementioned workbench and each time I enter the building I am assailed by twittering swallows that hover around my ears, no doubt questioning my right to be there. But when they selected this site, they didn't reckon on the cat! Who, being a nosey individual, didn't take long to discover them; and who I found on the bench, dancing on his hind legs and swatting at the swallows that dodged and ducked around him. The cat, in turn, hadn't reckoned on the effects of gravity and his gyrations became more frenzied as his frustration increased until he stepped clean of the edge of the bench and landed in an undignified heap on the concrete floor.

Having observed the demise of the cat I was sure that the swallows would be safe from his attentions but later that evening I witnessed an event that gave me cause for doubt. I'd gone to the window to close the curtains on the depleting day when I observed the maniacal cat, once again on his hind legs, running across the gravel driveway whilst madly swiping at something above his head. Suddenly, with a final lunge, he downed, from the air, what I imagined could only be a moth.

I rushed outside and discovered, to my astonishment, that this fearsome feline had, in fact, managed to catch a tiny pipistrelle in mid-flight. The minute, mouse-like mammal, with its outstretched, leathery wings, lay motionless on the gravel and, convinced that it was dead, I gathered it up and took it into the house to show the Doting Owner of the Spoilt Pony. She looked and 'oohed' and 'aahed' over the miniscule corpse and said 'poor little thing' or some such words and I left her with it. A few minutes later I could hear that her tone had changed. The previous cooings had gone up by several decibels and the reason? The pipistrelle wasn't dead, you see, only 'playing possum' and as she had carried it out of the house it had, like Lazarus, arisen from the dead and latched onto her finger with the hook- like projections on its 'elbows' – not something that most 'girlies' would enjoy!

Must go before you think I'm batty too!

August

Recently, we were enjoying a visit to a rather special garden that had been thrown open, albeit temporarily, to public access via the National Gardening Scheme when we happened upon a small graveyard where ten or fifteen dogs of yesteryear had been buried. Every grave was marked by a headstone or plaque of some description; each inscribed to the memory of a lost and, clearly, much loved pet. As we mulled over the various inscriptions we came across one that gave our heart strings a tug, *'died after months of suffering,'* it read. We looked at each other and wondered how someone could allow a treasured pet to suffer for months when we all have the warrant to make that painful decision, on behalf of our elderly or sick animals, when enough is enough.

The inscription was even more poignant to us for, just a few days beforehand, we had to make that heart-rending judgment on behalf of our lovely old Labrador, Jenny. Crippling arthritis and a weak chest had made life a burden and although it was upsetting at the time and her loss left a big void in our daily routine we are happy in the knowledge that she is now at peace.

But enough of such sorrowful ramblings; it's never been my intention to bring sadness to the pages of this superb publication. And, anyway, I have an important announcement to make so I'd better get on with it before I run out of space and my words become the victims of our erudite editors' pruning shears!

I've fallen in love!

There - I've said it and now you all know! And, I hear you ask, what sort of creature could turn the head of a man who's only been married for a mere eight months? Well, how does *young, big, bouncy* and *blonde*, with eyes to melt your heart and a face that says 'I love you too', grab you? Eh? And, what's even more amazing, the Doting Owner of the Spoilt Pony doesn't seem to mind at all!

His name is Buddy (I sincerely hope that <u>did</u> surprise you) and, by a pure quirk of fate, he came into our lives just a few days after dear old Jenny left us. A good friend, who is head keeper on a nearby estate, called to tell us that he had been asked to help in re-homing a nine-month old, golden, Labrador dog. Without any knowledge of our recent loss he had decided that we might be able to help and that is how, on the very next day, we collected Buddy from his distraught owner. The man clearly loved the dog and didn't want to part with him but circumstances dictated otherwise and we all had lumps in our throats as he handed over just about everything a much-loved dog could have.

My new love—*young, big, bouncy* and *blonde*

We took him home and made the necessary introductions to the rest of the household. My lovely spaniel, Maud, gave him a few educational 'nips' for getting too close to the love of her life, i.e. me! The geriatric Jack Russell dismissed him as we would an ill-behaved youth and the cat packed his bags and left home – but not for long. The chickens proved to be a source of delight until, that is, he was severely mugged by a crotchety old hen that had been chased once too often and a near-miss from a flying hoof dissuaded him from chasing the spoilt pony around the paddock.

But, notwithstanding his initial 'teething troubles' he is a good lad and this ménage now has a new and much welcomed member and I'm moved to wonder just how much effect fate, or whatever name you want to give it, has on all of our lives.

You must all think I'm barking!

September

You don't need me to tell you that we have had one of the wettest summers in living memory. In fact, the owner of the spoilt pony heard that from Good Friday up until 24th July we did not have two consecutive days without rainfall!! With the odds stacked so unfavourably it was nothing less than a small miracle that we managed to successfully hold two of our local, annual events.

With just about every outdoor show cancelled throughout the country (including the CLA Game Fair which must be one of the largest events in Europe) the organisers of The New Forest and Hampshire County Show were adamant that the *'show would go on'*. In the run-up to 24th July exhibitors and participants were threatened with a variety of unmentionable punishments for daring to drive on the hallowed grass and much effort was applied by all concerned in hand- carrying items that under normal conditions would be driven onto the site. So, with the sanity of the stalwart committee being questioned by many of us, the first day arrived and with it came the sun- in fact we cooked! Someone up there smiled down on us and around the fly fishing pool we baked in the unusually high temperatures. Sun block, shorts, hats and sun glasses became the order of the day and everyone began to enjoy the show.

On the Wednesday a smart helicopter flew low over the show ground and landed on the nearby polo pitch- Her Majesty the Queen together with Prince Philip had dropped in to pay us a visit. It was their last official engagement in the Jubilee Year and we were all very honoured that they had elected to come to the New Forest and how could anyone have considered cancelling the show with such important guests in the offing. It is with regret that I have to tell you that neither of the Royal visitors had put in a request to meet me but I did get to shake hands and have a chat with Alan Titchmarsh who was the President of the show this year.

But enough of all this wittering about the NF Show when there was an equally prestigious event in the offing. I speak of course of our very own Burley Village Show and once again the gods smiled down on the Manor Park and kept the rain at bay. To say there was a drying wind, however, would be an understatement. If you were there on the day then you'll remember that it blew and buffeted the marquees and pergolas relentlessly until one or two took off and relocated without permission. Casting a fly line in these conditions was almost impossible and I'm sure that most of the hundreds of visitors who passed by wondered just we were trying to achieve!

But did the windy conditions put any one off? Not at all. With true British spirit our show went on and everyone had a good time. Despite the appalling gardening year, the shows judges were treated to an amazing display of vegetables and flowers and all the other competitions were well supported with entries from many first-time entrants.

Poppy

The dog show was, as ever, well supported but I have to tell you that the winning dog – one Poppy, a little schnauzer – was not a local dog. She belonged to a couple who were staying with us and had travelled down from the Medway to steal our treasured prize. I did admonish them for their cheek but they didn't care- their little dog had won first prize!

So, to Dan Tanner, the show committee and all the behind-the-scene people please accept a big thank you for a job, once again, well done.

With all that and then the Olympic Games, what a wonderful year we are having.

You must all think I'm showing off!

October

I am often amazed by the misconceptions that some visitors seem to have about this lovely Forest of ours and none more than recently when, on one of the rare sunny mornings of the year, I had occasion to leave the Inclosure by a different route than was usual; a route which took me past the end of my own driveway. I was annoyed to see a small white van parked directly in front of the gate to the Inclosure and ultimately to my home. The drivers' door was open and on it, smoking a cigarette, leant a middle-aged man clothed in a pair of track suit bottoms and a white singlet. I stopped my car and got out with the intention of asking him to move his vehicle.

I bade him good morning and he returned the greeting. "I hope you're not thinking of stopping there" I said.

"You're too late, Mate. I've been here all night." He said all too quickly as he flicked his dog-end into the Forest and straightened himself up.

I pointed out to him that by sleeping in his vehicle anywhere other than in one of the camp sites was a contravention of Forest by-laws. This didn't seem to cause him any concern; instead he slammed the door and approached me in a belligerent manner.

"I don't think that's exactly a hanging offence – do you?" He said with his face close to mine.

It was apparent from his attitude that I could be in for a spot of bother from this thoroughly objectionable individual and decided to be a little more aggressive in my own approach. I advised Mr. Nasty that he was in fact blocking my right of way and therefore preventing access to my property. He glanced over his shoulder and looked down the winding, gravelled track before turning his attention back to me.

"Nah, I'm not having that" He mocked "No one lives in there. " He indicated the general direction of the Inclosure with a jerk of his balding head.

In retrospect, I'm sure that he was of the opinion that I was just being awkward but, for a moment, I was at a loss for words and struggling for a suitable reply when, just like the cavalry in the movies, the postman in his red van pulled up in a cloud of dust. Out jumped the 'Postie', oblivious to the row that was brewing between me and my new- found 'friend', with a handful of letters.

"Cor, what a luxury meeting you here, Ian". He grinned from ear to ear as he handed me the mail and addressing the complete stranger continued "You don't know just how much time it saves me if I don't have to drive all the way down to his house" and he too nodded in the direction of the Inclosure then turned and with a cheery wave of farewell jumped in his van and continued with his deliveries.

I turned to my antagonist who was staring open-mouthed after the departing postman. I didn't say a word-I didn't have to, the postman had said it all for me. He looked at me sheepishly and simply said "I guess I'll be moving then" and without further ado and with obvious embarrassment he hopped into his vehicle and followed the departing postman!

Despite the odd objectionable individual, most of our visitors are very pleasant and their naivety where Forest matters are concerned can sometimes be amusing and I'll quote the little girl who when passing our house found a dead squirrel that the cat had left outside the gate. She bent over and examined the stiffened corpse for quite a while before turning to her Mother and announcing in a profound voice,   "Hamster not breathing."

Must go – I'm out of breath too

The Forestry
Commission
Byelaws 1962

November

Not so long ago we lost a dear friend and the Forest lost a real character. Bill was a man who lived his life as he saw fit, but on the way he passed-on an enormous amount of knowledge, for those who could be bothered to listen, about Forest skills and country life. I am pleased to say that I spent many an informative day with him either in a pigeon hide or working ferrets in woodland and hedgerows and I learnt more about country ways, during those all too brief interludes, than I could possibly learn from a book or TV programme. It's true that he wasn't always totally within the law in everything he did, for he had his own theories on what was right and what was wrong but he was a kindly man who never bore a grudge or had any desire to harm a soul. I'm sure he wouldn't mind me describing him as a likeable rogue who was blessed with a wicked sense of humour; he took great delight in making others laugh with his many stories – and this is one of them.

Bill and his loader 2005

Many years ago, when the village Bobby knew everybody on his patch, Bill was erecting a new fence for the owner of a Forest property. Whilst he went about his work, his venerable and somewhat dishevelled truck was parked outside the premises, on the highway. He was so engrossed with what he was doing that he didn't notice the local policeman approaching on his bicycle until he had stopped and dismounted. Bill observed him as he parked his bike against the hedge and, without a word, walked slowly around the vehicle giving it a thorough appraisal until, eventually, he approached Bill and enquired if the vehicle was his. Bill confessed that he was indeed the owner of the truck and the man in blue asked if he wouldn't mind switching on the lights which Bill, who wanted to stay on the right side of the law, did without question. The policeman walked around the rear of the truck and pointing to the back of the vehicle advised our hero that one of the side lights wasn't working. Bill followed the policeman's pointing finger and agreed with him that the light was not illuminated as, indeed, it should've been.

Without further ado, he politely pushed the Bobby to one side and, swinging his leg back, delivered a hefty kick with his mud-encrusted boot which struck the offending light with a mighty blow.   The light, in deference to this brutal treatment, came on and old Bill stood back to admire his handy work.   He was pleased with the outcome of his somewhat rustic approach to vehicle maintenance and he looked up with a smile to observe the policemans' reaction.

Clearly, the village Bobby was not impressed by the result of Bills' ministrations. He stood for a while looking straight into Bills grinning face and then, without a word, he strolled casually to the front of the truck and turned to look at the windscreen. He studied the muddied glass for several minutes and then beckoned Bill to come and stand beside him. Bill, with some trepidation, did as requested for he knew that not everything was in order at that end of the truck. The policeman put a friendly arm around his shoulder and looking down at him with a wry grin he pointed at the vehicle and said;

"Now try kicking the windscreen too and see if that'll bring your tax disc up to date!!"

> That made Bill laugh - I hope it made you chuckle too!

December

The original part of this lovely, old cottage which stands deep within the inclosure, according to a stone set in the wall, was constructed in 1811 and I have often wondered why and indeed how it was built up here in the middle of nowhere and, having spent the greater part of my life in the construction industry, I for one, can really appreciate the logistical problems of building a dwelling, in those days of yore, in such a remote location.

Burley Rails Cottage 1811

I imagine that the first task would have been to dig the well, by hand, of course; for without water it would have been impossible to mix the mortar with which to lay the bricks. All construction materials e.g. bricks, lime, sand, tiles, timber, etc. would have been laboriously transported by horse and cart which would have been loaded and unloaded by hand and the

ability to jump in a van and pop down to the Builders Merchant for a few
forgotten nails or screws was definitely not an option. So why then go to
all that trouble and effort to build such a dwelling in the heart of the
Forest?

The answer came from a document which was shown to me, recently, by
our retired keeper Derek Gulliver and it transpires that in the early 1800's
orders were set out to appoint a number of woodmen whose duty it would
be to look after the inclosures. And it was for these men and their
families that a number of cottages were constructed, in or near those
inclosures, throughout the Forest. Although a much respected member of
Forest society, the woodman's lot was not an easy one. For a wage of 12/
- (60p!!) a week he was responsible for the felling, planting and thinning
of the inclosures around his cottage; together with the upkeep of fences,
drains, gates, roads, bridges and bunnies. He was expected to report and
investigate any trespass against the woods and to '*give up the whole of his
time to his job*'!! Furthermore, he could not take leave without prior
permission and if he should be dismissed, for any reason, from his
position, he would not be entitled to a gratuity.

With each cottage came a small parcel of land; a quarter acre of which
was set aside as a nursery for young trees. Another quarter acre was
intended for the growing of vegetables for his own use and the remainder
consisted of a small paddock where he was allowed to keep one cow.
However, in the mid 1800's L. H. Cumberbatch, the Deputy Surveyor,
generously decided that woodmen should also be allowed to keep a pony;
but only on the condition that it was available for services to the Crown!
This meant that whilst the poor woodman eventually had transport in his
often remote cottage, the good, old Crown got the benefit of the use a
horse and cart at no additional cost!!

On the basis that growing crops on the paddock would take up time that
the employee should be spending on his job, it was forbidden to plough
and cultivate the paddocks and one woodman, who was caught doing just
that, was suspended for three or four days and then relocated to another
cottage with a smaller plot! To add insult to injury, his pay was docked
for the period of suspension.

When the Inclosures were eventually 'thrown open' some of the cottages
were either totally demolished or taken down and re-erected near another,
new inclosure. Why this cottage was not, ultimately, demolished is not
clear but records show that it was sold into private ownership in 1971 for
the princely sum of £4260.00!! And I thank my lucky stars that it was.

Have a very happy Christmas.

January

Can you believe it? Another year has gone by. Where does time go? But what a year it was; a Diamond Jubilee celebration and the London, 2012 Olympics and, of course, the weather!! You don't need me to tell you that we have just experienced the wettest summer for a hundred years and, as you are all aware, the rain is still with us as I write!! But did you know that in April, despite the fact that it was the wettest April on record, seven water companies across southern and eastern England brought in hosepipe bans after two unusually dry winters left some groundwater supplies and rivers as low as in the drought year of 1976! But, lucky old us, the restrictions were followed by record rainfall, most of which, I am sure, fell on this New Forest of ours, in that same month, followed by even more rain in May and June which, I know you will be relieved to hear led to the hosepipe bans being lifted in June and July so feel free to water the garden or fill the swimming pool if, indeed, you are minded!

Autumn colours at Mouse's Cupboard

Heavy rainfall can be a trial for those who live in low-lying areas but up here on Woolfield Hill the greatest inconvenience to us was caused by the torrents of rain water that ran down the track from the top of the hill, straight under the gates and fences to finally sulk on the lawn and paddocks. The free-range chickens had a great time scratching and paddling in the mud until, that is, their range was restricted when I decided that enough was enough and confined them to a temporary pen. I suspect that it will take a long time before the bare mud patches that they have created on the lawn, recover. Similarly, the spoilt pony was cutting-up her paddocks and, whilst I did consider issuing her with galoshes, the Doting Owner sensibly confined her, whenever possible, to the stable yard and treated her to more than her normal share of outings onto the Forest.

This unprecedented rainfall has been a disaster for our farmers and for the Forest in general. As the fields lay sodden and untillable across the area, in many barns autumn sowings of barley and grass seed remain in their sacks and the Forest is empty and bare. The wild, Autumn harvest is almost non-existent; wild fungi peeped above ground for a brief spell when the weather was more amenable and then decided that discretion was the better part of valour and refused to show when it turned again. Crab apples are scarce, although I'm glad to report that we did find enough to replenish the larder with several jars of their delicious jelly, acorns, beech mast, chestnuts, holly berries, rowan berries, rose hips and just about anything else that helps to sustain our wildlife are just as scarce and, in consequence, the Forest is empty. This dearth of food resulted in an insignificant deer rut this year and my tasty wood pigeons haven't shown either.

But 'it's an ill wind that blows nobody any good' and the grass has continued to grow and grow and the Forest ponies and cattle look fat and nourished and ready to take whatever the next few months throw at them. And what an autumn! Did you ever see such magnificent colours as there were this year? Up here in the Inclosure we were treated, albeit all too briefly, to a display of red, yellow, brown and gold foliage as the trees prepared to undress for winter.

Must go now and sweep up some more leaves; but before I do, may I wish you all, from all of us up here in the Inclosure, a very happy and prosperous New Year.

February

Not so long ago, on yet another filthy day, when the rain tipped endlessly from the sky, I was with a colleague in the depths of an exceedingly spiteful bog - just minding our own business, you understand - when my pal, who was facing me, looked over my shoulder and nodded to indicate something behind. I turned, half expecting to see an unusual bird or perhaps a deer, but to my amazement, there on the edge of a prickly, Blackthorn spinney, almost hub-deep in the mire, I spotted a couple of cyclists. And what a pathetic sight they were! Clad in matching, body-hugging, bright, yellow outfits that were spattered with indelible, peaty, brown mud whilst, on their heads, they wore substantial helmets with what appeared to be Teletubbie-type appendages. They made an odd looking couple in that wild environment and, as the male member of the duo eased, with a squelch, a leg from the cloying ooze, he exposed ankle socks and dainty, leather shoes the colour of which matched the aforementioned outfits. They were, clearly, both inadequately dressed and lost and without further ado I wandered in their direction to offer some help.

They looked at me, open-mouthed, as I wished them a Good Morning and advised them that cycling on the Forest was restricted to gravel tracks. I suggested that they follow my directions to the nearest track, from where they could continue their journey. The male member of the pair confessed that they knew nothing of the cycling by-law whilst his female counterpart continued to look me up and down with a little too much curiosity for my liking! They were, however, very polite and cooperative and with a farewell 'thanks' they plodded off in the general direction of Bolderwood.

I returned to my companion and told him that they were a strange looking couple to meet in this neck of the woods. He reckoned that they probably thought much the same about me and advised me to give some thought to my own appearance, which I did. Green Wellie's, cammo trousers and jacket – oh, and a gun! Nothing strange about that, is there? He said there was nothing unusual with that unless, of course, you hail from one of the major conurbations where anyone in similar dress would result in a Calling out of the Guard, the SAS, The Special Response Unit, Old Uncle Tom Cobleigh and all!! He went on to say that I looked like a walking tree and that I was probably on U-tube, whatever that is, - in my day it was a bend under the kitchen sink!! But no, it is, apparently, an 'on-line site' (in my day - a railway station) where people are free to publish their videos; you see it seems that the Teletubbie appendages were, in fact, video cameras. Oh well, I always wanted to be on the big screen!

Strange looking local writer, with dogs

And the point of all this rambling? Now we are a National Park, whether you like it or not, we do have and will continue to have more and more visitors. And they have every right to come here, and they are beneficial to the local economy but, if this Forest is to survive this ever increasing footfall, then **education** is the order of the day. Many of these visitors come from such disparate walks of life that they have no inkling of what makes our Forest tick. They have no idea about our way of life and the designation *National Park,* to some of them, means National Playground. We can't blame cyclists for going 'off- piste' if they know no better; any more than we can point a finger at those who park in gateways or feed the animals, when they shouldn't. At one time the Forest by-laws were common knowledge but few, now, are aware of their very existence. So come on Forestry Commission, National Park Authority or whoever! Make a New Year resolution and give them some education before it's too late and the very place that they've come to see and where we all love to live, is ruined forever.

Time I got off my own bike!

March

Back in 2009 I wrote, in this erudite magazine, a few words about God's Gate which is located on the boundary of North Oakley Inclosure. It's an ancient wicket gate that hangs on remarkable, hand-forged hinges next to a shiny, new, five-bar gate; both of which guard the Southern end of Sandy Ridge, a gravel track that stretches across the open Forest until it terminates at the noisy and smelly A31. I told of the hand-carved legend that I'd discovered, fixed to the underside of the top rail of this elderly example of Forest furniture, which read 'ALL THIS BEAUTY IS OF GOD'. I went on to relate how some mindless individual had chosen to deface the carving, probably with a knife, until it was illegible and how saddened I was for the unknown person who had taken the trouble to create and install the sign. I promised, in 2009, that I would fashion a new version of the legend and fix it alongside the original and that's just what I did. And that, or so you would think, would be the end of it– but it wasn't!!

Gods Gate

A couple of years after I had replaced the carving, it was wrenched from the gate and discarded nearby.   Perhaps, I thought, I had offended someone by duplicating the original but, nonetheless, after a few days I returned and re-fixed the legend, this time, with two really hefty screws. And there it remained for quite a while until in 2012 it disappeared altogether – the only evidence of it ever having been there was a long, bent, wood screw in the underside of the rail.   By now I was really puzzled but, undaunted and feeling just a bit obstinate, I did no more than make and fix a replacement which, I'm pleased to say has, for the moment, remained unscathed.

My tale continues when, late in 2012, I received a letter from the person who claims responsibility for the original inscription which, apparently, was fixed there on 13th September 1979. The writer gives no explanation or reason for creating the plaque; the wording of which, I've since discovered, is the motto of the Isle of Wight! The letter goes on to explain that the author had spotted my original article, about Gods Gate, in my book 'From a New Forest Inclosure' and had been prompted to correspond with me. The writer refers to Gods Gate as '*my gatelet*' and was '*delighted to see on 5th Aug 2010 that some kind person had made and fitted beside it,* (the original sign) *a slightly larger sign, much better and easy to read.*' So, clearly, my actions over the past few years had not antagonised the originator of the inscription who goes on to say '*I was disappointed however to find on 17th Feb 2011 that the new sign was missing, but it was back in place when I passed a few weeks later. On 2 Aug 2012 once again it was missing. My perplexity is boundless!*' 'And so is mine because, despite the fact that he or she has been kind enough to write to me, the letter is unsigned and there is no address to reply to! Mysterious or what?

I'm sure that the anonymous writer has good reason for remaining so, but the story doesn't quite end here. You see the Doting Owner was riding her Spoilt Pony, just recently, when they came upon Gods Gate and there, resting on top of the gate, was my first remake that had inexplicably disappeared, so many months ago! Now that is mystifying!!

Must go, I'm feeling rather odd, myself!

April

It is, now, that time of the year when we concentrate our efforts in an attempt to reduce the numbers of those grey, North American invaders that cause so much damage in our plantations and predate, in the spring, on the eggs and chicks of our wild birds. I write, of course, about the grey squirrel; a creature for which I don't have a lot of praise nor do the woodsmen and keepers who, over the years, have done their damndest to protect this Forest from these yellow-toothed rodents. In the period from the end of January until the start of the Easter holidays we have, annually, waged war on this arboreal enemy and, traditionally, with a modicum of success. I wish I could tell you that this year had been no different – but I can't – they've gone, vanished, done a bunk, emigrated – who knows?
But it's a fact; there are very few squirrels in the Forest at the moment.

Drey poking

It's at this point that I know some of the readers of this magazine will be tearing their hair out in disbelief and frustration; their hands will be hovering over the phone as they search for my number to tell me just what a fool I am! And I can't blame them, for I know that many of them are being seriously troubled by these gum-chewing, tree rats but take it from me or ask any of our Crown Keepers, if you prefer, and they will tell you just the same – there are very few squirrels in the woods and plantations, at the moment, and here, I think, is the reason why.

Last year, if you remember, the Good Lord decided, in his infinite wisdom, to re-enact the Great Flood. I don't know if he remembered the bit about forty days and forty nights or whether he was just trying something different but you don't need me to tell you that, in fact, it rained for most of the year! And we are still living with the after effects as I write, which brings me back, in a roundabout way, to the pesky squirrels.

You see the Forest trees, which had stood for weeks with their feet submersed in water and, at the same time suffering some pretty miserable weather, decided that enough was enough and threw a tantrum. They agreed, almost unanimously, that they wouldn't introduce off-spring into such a wet and miserable world and the net result was a non-existent, autumn harvest in 2012. No acorns or beech mast, chestnuts so skinny they wouldn't feed a mouse and a dearth of berries generally. What was a self-respecting, hungry squirrel to do? Well, I'll tell you. They upped sticks and moved, that's what they did and, not only that, they moved straight into our gardens and onto our bird feeders where we so generously feed them. Urban gardens, however, are not the only locations that were invaded; their numbers have also increased in the towns around the Forest where the nice, kind bunnie-huggers feed them in the parks and open spaces. Shooting estates within the Forest and on the fringes are also recording large numbers of squirrels which have been, all season and still are, taking full advantage of the food that is intended for the pheasants and partridges. It's not just the food they steal that makes them so unpopular, it's also the damage they inflict on feed containers, equipment and property generally with their long, sharp teeth.

But take heart! If the snow that I'm watching out of the window clears off!! and the weather becomes more seasonal, then our peanuts will get some respite when the 'skuggies' come marching back into the Forest to munch the young, tender, tree buds that they love so much; safe in the knowledge that we won't be shooting them again until the holiday season is over!!

Must go and squirrel away some cartridges for the autumn!

May

Over the years we and our forebears have been guilty of inflicting some serious damage to our flora and fauna. The introduction of alien species, whether intentional or by inadvertent escapism, has caused the decline and even extinction of many animals, plants and birds. My arch enemy the grey squirrel, which has had a devastating effect on our native red squirrel population, is a classic example; so, too, is that other American invader, the mink, which has populated our rivers and streams, having been released from fur farms by well intentioned but ignorant 'bunny huggers', causing a disastrous decline in the numbers of our delightful little water voles and fish stocks. And it doesn't end there, oh no! Muntjac deer are destroying our bluebell woods, ring-necked parakeets are wreaking havoc around the streets and parks in London, terrapins and bull frogs are chomping our fish whilst Indian or Himalayan Balsam is marching steadily along our waterways, relentlessly choking our native vegetation as it goes. The list goes on and I'm not going to bore you with more examples; but it's no wonder, with this abundance of unusual species, that errors in identification can occur.

Culled Ring-necked Parakeets

Let me tell you a little story that will illustrate one such mistake.   There once was a lovely lady who lived in the centre of Southampton, within easy walk of the high street with its shops and all the conveniences that you would associate with city life. If she was still with us, she would be the first to admit that she was an out and out 'Townie' and extremely comfortable with her lot until, that is, she met and married her husband, a Countryman by any other name, who dragged her away from her life within the city streets and into a totally new environment, here in our beautiful New Forest.

Now, the lady in question, was a sensible woman and, once she had recovered from the shock of such an extreme change in lifestyle, she adopted the 'if you can't beat them then join them' philosophy and set about the task of familiarising herself with country life. She immediately took riding lessons and soon became a competent horsewoman and horse owner; she followed her husband in his many country pursuits and took note of everything that was going on around her. And, slowly but surely, she learned the names of many of the birds and animals that she encountered in her new life.

It became her habit, each morning before she set off to work in the big city, to walk her dogs in the woods that surrounded her new home. On one such morning she returned home in a state of great excitement and, finding her husband talking to the New Forest keeper on whose beat she lived, announced that she had just encountered a huge **skunk!!** The husband and the keeper looked at each other in amazement as she went on to explain that the dogs had disturbed it and harried it from some bushes, whereupon it had headed straight towards her, stopping only a yard or so from her feet before charging off in the opposite direction. The husband asked her to describe the creature and she replied that it was big and black with white stripes. He reached for a book and turned the pages until he found what he was looking for which, of course, was a picture of a badger. She looked at the illustration and blushed with embarrassment and apologised for her stupidity and ignorance. The keeper, who was a kindly man, disagreed with her by saying that he could never think of her as a stupid woman but would always remember her as the only person, ever, who had spotted a skunk in the New Forest!!

Must go now - before I make a mistake, too.

June

I don't want to be found guilty of tempting providence but I think we've made it!! At long last, spring seems to have arrived!! Through the window of my study I can see the beech trees are now in full leaf and the oaks are hurrying to catch them up. The view down the grass ride to the Burley/Bolderwood track is now obscured by a wall of green – hurrah!! The little chiff-chaffs and the not-so-little cuckoos, both harbingers of spring, have been chiff-chaffing and cuckooing for some while now and, all around, the garden birds are showing signs of nesting. The Mandarin ducks are, once again, visiting the pond but the drake is, more often than not, alone on the water; so I reckon his mate is already sitting on a clutch of eggs high up in one of the ancient trees in the neighbouring Forest. Blackbirds, some of our earliest nesters, have mated and several pairs spend all their day on the lawn searching for and gathering food for their hungry chicks. A pied wagtail and her mate are nesting in the ivy beside the patio doors which hasn't gone unnoticed by the cat! – I wish them luck! And, meanwhile, Mr and Mrs Swallow have returned from their holiday in Africa and spend much of their time on the bars in the stable chattering away to each other. I'm sure that they are surveying their nests of previous years and trying to decide on whether it will be a new-build or a refurbishment job this year!

The chickens and the bantams have also been infected with spring fever and some time ago one of the little bantam hens decided to 'go broody' on eighteen eggs. The Doting Owner of the Spoilt Pony duly noted the date and her head filled with visions of fluffy chicks in abundance. As time went on, the fussy, Mother-to-be rejected an egg, then another; which was followed by another and yet another, until finally, about a dozen eggs remained. On the duly reckoned 21st day the Doting Owner hurried down to the kitchen garden, where the bantam coop was located, to see what she would see. But it wasn't her eyes that made her heart flip; it was her ears that detected, before she arrived at the gate, the unmistakeable cheeping of a new born chick. With her eyes fixed firmly and expectantly on the wire run which was some twenty feet away, she opened the gate to the vegetable garden and promptly trod on the first of her future stock which had, somehow, escaped from the run and was immediately inside the gate. She was devastated by her unfortunate accident and went on to discover another dead chick inside the coop that had, unfortunately, fallen from the nest box during the cold night and, unable to regain the protective warmth of the hen, had succumbed to the unseasonably low temperature.

Undaunted by these misfortunes, the resolute little bird sat on her remaining eggs for a further forty-eight hours until it was obvious that they were infertile. Undeterred by her lack of success, the would be Chicken Farmer placed a clutch of eggs from our Rhode Island/Sussex cross hens under the still-broody, bantam and another 21 days went by

Bantam and chick

until, at last, success! Well, success of sorts – only one chick hatched from the entire bunch but it was healthy and lively and the little hen looked after it; and it thrived and grew and feathers began to replace the downy fluff of birth when disaster struck again – the mother bantam died! There was no explanation for her sudden demise but our single chick is now an orphan. It was my idea to name it 'Lonely' but this was rejected by the 'Chicken Farmer' in favour of a name more suited to its birthday which was on 5th April and so now little *'Year End'* is part of our ménage.

Must go now –before I get hen-pecked!

July

Those of you who have nothing better to do than read my ramblings will know that I am often bemused by the way that some of our visitors conceive this beautiful Forest of ours and how it functions; and I met a man the other day who did nothing to dissuade my conviction that there are certain people, not necessarily visitors, who have, to say the least, an unusual perception of some aspects of Forest life.

Ragwort

The man in question is an old friend and a 'Forester born and bred' who lives near Marchwood and who worked, before he took retirement, in Fawley refinery. He told me about a fellow refinery employee who was a self-confessed 'Townie' with, nonetheless, a high regard for the Hampshire countryside and a desire to learn as much about it as he could. In consequence of which, he was continually questioning my pal about the various things he observed during his journey, to and from work. One day, at about this time of year, he asked about the vibrant fields of yellow that he had recently observed in fields just north of Romsey and was duly advised that what he had seen were crops of oilseed rape; and that, or so my colleague thought, was that.

Several weeks went by until, on a warm summer day, the 'Townie', driving across the Forest, spotted several young Foresters who were industriously employed in pulling the poisonous, yellow ragwort from the roadside verges. On arriving at his place of work he announced that oilseed rape must be very valuable and, when asked why he could possibly have such a thought, he went on to explain that he had seen several people pulling it, bagging it and carting it away by lorry –'and, if it wasn't valuable, they wouldn't be collecting it, would they?'

But it's not only visitors and 'Townies' who can create a howler. My old friend went on to tell me about the signs that suddenly appeared, not so long ago, on the grass verges in the Ipley Cross area of the Forest. He couldn't remember the exact wording but they read something akin to '*DO NOT MOW – CONSERVATION AREA*'. They were, apparently, purposed-made signs and had, no doubt, been funded from public coffers. I cannot think that this blunder was made by the Forestry Commission and I'll leave it to your own imaginations to guess who the perpetrators of this signage might have been! But when all is said and done, there is someone out there, in a position of some authority, who perhaps believes, as do many of our visitors, that there is an army of little men who come out in the hours of darkness with strimmers and ride-on mowers to carefully groom the Forests' verges and lawns. But hold on! Maybe I do this person an injustice. Perhaps he or she is well-aware that the animals are 'the architects of the Forest' but is under the misguided opinion that the ponies, cattle and deer can read!!

I have to tell you that having written the foregoing, I was driving back from Crow when my passage was obstructed by a thumping great tractor with an hydraulic arm extended from its near-side; on the end of which, hovering above the already close-cropped verge, was a madly spinning mower! What on earth is going on?

Must go now –before I get mown down too!

August

I'm sure I've mentioned before that Mother Nature has a way of balancing her books and, in the last few days, she hasn't let me down. I know that things are not as they should be in the natural world and that many species are becoming extremely rare or have, sadly, vanished from the face of the Earth but, just lately, after a few days of sunshine, this old Forest of ours is suddenly beginning to come alive!

Mint Beetle

It wasn't so long ago that I was discussing the dearth of butterflies and insects with a very knowledgeable chum who was convinced that the situation was irreversible; but he wasn't reckoning on old Mother Nature and, only yesterday, we stood together and looked down a sun-dappled ride and revelled in the sight of several species that neither of us had seen, so far, this year. In the garden, I've noticed hoverflies in abundance – something I haven't seen for several years and on the mint the stunning, emerald-green mint beetles are happily chomping their way through the foliage; these delightful insects are, apparently, quite rare and if you are fortunate to find them on your mint plants then don't despair; just think yourself lucky and grow a bit more mint so there's enough for both you and the beetles.

The birds, of course, are taking advantage of this bountiful harvest of insects and the pair of wagtails that were nesting in the ivy beside the patio doors gave us hours of pleasure as they bobbed about on the lawn; running after or, occasionally, jumping up to catch any low flying insects. The cat soon got fed-up with trying to catch these agile birds on the open expanse of the lawn and took to sneaky ambushes from below the barbeque on which they often landed before diving into the depths of the ivy. The wagtails were unperturbed by his futile attacks and treated him with so much disdain that I'm sure his pride as a hunter took a severe beating.

The seasonal weather prompted our remaining bantam to sit on a clutch of fifteen eggs and, unlike her sister who sadly died leaving the unfortunate orphan 'Year End' (who I told you about in June) to fend for himself, she managed to hatch thirteen chicks – not a good number if you happen to be superstitious and, yes, sadly, the inevitable 'runt' died and the cat chomped another, which left eleven (I was always good at maths!). Now, this particular bantam proved to be an excellent mother; always alert and ready to defend her brood if anyone dared to come to close but I think the sun must have upset her hormonal balance! Suddenly, before her brood were anywhere near fledged, she gave them all a severe pecking and trotted off to the lower paddock where her 'husband' had taken up residence with the now fully fledged and extremely ugly 'Year End'. There ensued a session of vociferous accusation and recrimination and much chasing about and feather rattling until, as the daylight began to fade, the brazen hussy was found, tucked up on a perch, between the bantam cock and 'Year End': the net result of which is that she is now laying a new clutch of eggs and the Doting Owner of The Spoilt Pony is keeping the deserted chicks in a coop until they reach a size that will not fit into the cats mouth!

Seriously though, isn't it delightful to have all this fabulous weather after so many months of abject misery. Our garden that, for the first time in memory, flooded - not bad when you live on the side of a hill - has now dried-out and for the first time in many months I've had to put the hose in the pond to restore its dwindling depths.

Must go now, before they slap on a hose ban!!

September

It was announced this morning that the Government intends to inject £94m into the economy in order to promote cycling. Eight major conurbations will share £77m of this with the remaining £17m being allocated to four National Parks namely, The South downs, the Peak District, Dartmoor and yes, us, here in the New Forest. This is marvellous news for cyclists and those of us who are involved with or rely on tourism for an income and, now that we have the dubious status of National Park, we must expect a greater influx of visitors, many of whom will be cyclists. The Government says that the money is to improve existing and fund new cycle routes. Manchester alone will get £20m to build or improve some 30 miles of cycle paths and create new 20mph speed limit zones around the city. Major improvements to 93 miles of cycle routes on Dartmoor are anticipated. But what is going to be done to improve the lot of the cyclist in the New Forest?

Children cycling in the Inclosure

The on-line, 'Official visitor site' for the New Forest advises the visitors that there are in excess of 100 miles of marked cycle routes available to would be pedal pushers and, in an area of only 144 square miles, I think that's very generous. The site goes on to outline the concise, New Forest Cycling Code and warns those who might wish to cycle 'off-piste' that they could be subjected to a fine of up to £500.00 for doing so; which is all very sensible and commendable. But what about this newly acquired stash of money? Is it going to be used to create cycle lanes on our already overcrowded and narrow lanes and by- ways? I don't think so but something needs to be done before we have more injuries and heaven forbid fatalities on our Forest roads.

You may wonder why I'm prattling on about cyclists and I can assure you that I have nothing against those (and they are the majority) who are sensible, Forest friendly and safe but, recently, I have been scared out of my wits by cyclists. I was driving past a family group, part of which was a tiny tot on an equally tiny bike who was peddling for all he was worth to keep up. I gave the group a very wide berth as I passed them but was horrified to see the little boys' tiny crash helmet within inches of my passenger window as he wobbled right across the highway. Fortunately I missed him, or I should say he missed me! On another occasion I was following a horse box when we came upon two cyclists with numbers on their backs. Clearly they were in some sort of race and as the horse box passed them one of the cyclists decided to overtake his colleague and, in doing so, swerved into the side of the trailer. Fortunately no one was hurt but it was a near thing. I don't wish to be an old grouch but are our narrow lanes the right place for tiny tots or organised races? Perhaps the money could be spent on education!

On a lighter note and still cycle related, the mowers have been out again and they've mown the verges within our Inclosure on a hit and miss basis – very strange! The sides of the tracks have been mown for several yards and then been left for a while and then mown again. Now, the Doting Owner of the Spoilt Pony is a woman with a curious nature and she enquired of a passing Ranger the reason for this unusual phenomenon. She was told that it was to prevent the wild animals from jumping out on unsuspecting cyclists. What a good idea, but I hope they have warned the wild animals that they are only allowed to jump out where the verges have been mown and not where they have been left untouched!!

Must go now – it's recycling day!

October

I'm sure you'll all agree that since the longest day, or thereabouts, we have enjoyed a pretty spectacular summer and wherever we look we can see the results, some good and some not so good, of this marvellous weather. Out on the Forest everything that grows seems to have benefitted from the sunshine and the autumn harvest is all set to be a memorable one. Crab apples, blackberries, rowan berries, and hazel nuts are there for the picking and the branches of the oak tree that stands outside my study window are sagging under the weight of acorns and, just next to it, an elderly beech tree is positively groaning with its load of mast. Hopefully, this natural bounty will fatten the deer and, perhaps, this year, they'll have a decent rut; can there be any sounds more typical of this Forest or more evocative than the grunting stags or the belching bucks? With luck, tasty woodpigeon and wild ducks will flock from far and wide to feast on the acorns and, some, I hope, will end up in our freezer! However, the plethora of acorns will not be welcomed by those of you who keep horses or ponies; these fruits, that provide so much nourishment to other creatures, are lethal if consumed in quantity by horses and, consequently, the doting owner of the spoilt pony is fretting in anticipation of the thousands of acorns that will have to be cleared, in the weeks to come, from the perimeters of our paddocks.

The kitchen garden has, all in all, been very successful; the peas have produced bigger yields than I can ever remember and the onions and shallots have cropped so well that they should see us through until next year. Carrots, runner beans, broad beans and all plants that go into a good salad have kept us going for weeks, but there is one section of the garden that is looking really sad.

Do you remember how pleased I was to report, in the August edition of this learned publication, the re-appearance of many species of butterflies? Well, I take it all back! And I'll tell you why! Just come and have a look at our brassica's – that's cabbages, generally, for the not so learned – they've not just been devoured, they've been decimated by the horrible, black and yellow caterpillars of the very cabbage white butterflies that I was raving about in August!! For a starter they tucked in to, of all things, the swedes and, when they'd reduced everything above ground to nothing more than bare ribs, they moved on to a main course of savoy and greyhound cabbages and now, to add insult to injury, for their pud, they're chomping through the purple sprouting broccoli!! All attempts to dissuade them from destroying our plants are in vain. We've tried spraying them;

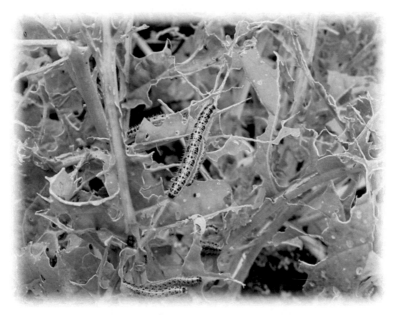

Caterpillar of the Cabbage White Butterfly

but the sun-aroused adults simply mate and lay more eggs which, within a few hours, hatch into more of the leaf-chomping larvae; we've both wasted hours of our time in picking them off, one by one, but still they reproduce faster than we can pick. We even tried feeding them to the chickens and bantams who rushed over excitedly when they saw something being thrown for them; but, clearly, they don't eat this particular insect for they backed-off in horror when they saw what was offered. So great are the numbers of these ravenous creatures, and no, I'm not paranoid, that I swear, when all else is quiet, I can hear the sound of their collective mastication!!

In truth, we've now given up with our fight against these crop devouring maggots but next year, as suggested by our farrier, spring greens will be the preferred crop which, hopefully, will be done and dusted and in our tummies before the butterflies put in an appearance!

I wonder if the farrier could 'shoe' them off!

November

I quote from the 'birdwatch' web site: '*Most birders probably have a mental list of their favourite birds but, if they had an equivalent one for their most frustrating, I bet Goshawk Accipiter Gentilis would feature quite highly. Despite the fact that it has increased significantly in Britain in recent years, it remains difficult to see*', Well let me tell you Matey, whoever you are who wrote that, if any of your frustrated readers want to see a goshawk then all they've got to do is pop down to our house, here in the New Forest, and they'll be able to get 'up-close and personal' with one

Gosshawk on a Rhode Island Red

A week or two ago the Doting Owner of the Spoilt Pony and would-be chicken farmer noticed that one of her bantams was missing and, quite naturally, she laid the blame, fairly and squarely, at the door of Charlie Fox; until, that is, one of our guests, a few days later, told how she had seen a buzzard take yet another bantam from the ancient woodland beyond our boundary. When told of this sighting, I was sceptical; buzzards are not renowned as woodland hunters and my thoughts immediately focused on the possibility that it could, in fact, be a goshawk. The very next day another bantam did a vanishing trick and this time I managed to find, in the lower paddock and on the edge of the trees, a poignant scattering of feathers to mark her passing. The presence of a marauding goshawk was becoming more of a reality! A week or so went by without further incident and the chickens and bantams continued to roam in peace until, - wait for it -, the murderer struck again and this time there was no mistaking its identity.   Another visitor, an experienced 'birder', was beside himself with delight when he told me that he had spotted, not an hour before, his very first goshawk; the only problem being that it was on our lawn and was in the process of dining-out on one of our large Rhode Island/Light Sussex, laying hens!! There was no mistaking his sighting for he produced both a photograph of the raptor on the aforementioned lawn and an old, paper, feed bag, wherein was the shredded corpse of the hapless hen.

Now I'm a keen birdwatcher, as most of you will know, and the goshawk is a superb piece of powerful, aerodynamic, hunting machinery; similar in size to a buzzard, but with the ability to fly at speed through woodland and forest, it is a highly efficient killer.   The text books tell us that because of persecution and deforestation it became all-but extinct, in this country, about two hundred years ago, until, that is, some bright sparks decided, in the 1970's, to re-introduce the species. Now here's the rub! These goshawk-huggers couldn't find any British birds – well, they were extinct, weren't they, so they trotted over to Finland and brought back the next best thing – or so they thought. The Scandinavian goshawks are much larger than our original native species; in fact they are thumping-great brutes but, notwithstanding this, they settled down and began to breed and, of course, to hunt and feed.

Now, things have changed during the past two hundred years and the wisdom in importing these super-killers into our Forest of today, has to be questioned – is there enough food for them?   Will they be as successful as the red kite and become a nuisance to many? Only time will tell.

But, what next? We've made some awful faux-pas over the last century or so and the spread of the grey squirrel and the demise of our native red is a prime example. Perhaps the re-introduction of the grey wolf or the brown bear would be a good idea? At least, that would, perhaps, go some way to resolving the wiggling, cyclist dilemna!!

Be very, very careful out there!

December

I listened to the weather forecast on Sunday 27th October which predicted strong winds gusting up to one hundred miles per hour but I wasn't that bothered; it was, surely, another, 'Michael effect' a term that has been coined, following that ill-fated prediction by Michael fish in 1987, whereby British weathermen are now inclined to predict 'a worst-case scenario' in order to avoid being caught out.

As the morning went on the warnings from the Met Office increased alarmingly. So, was this yet another 'Michael effect' or were we really in for a blow? I was uneasy about the whole thing and conscious of the fact that our generator had, after many years of service, died and gone to that great scrap yard in the sky and, more to the point, the space that it had occupied, in my workshop, remained empty! After a quick look on the internet and a few phone calls it became obvious that generators were being snapped-up across Southern England and so, without further ado, I gathered-up the Doting Owner of the Spoilt Pony and we trundled-off to a nearby tool warehouse wherein, after parting with a considerable amount of 'folding stuff', we purchased a near-replica of the old generator that had served us so well over the preceding years.

A few hours later and after reading many instructions and wielding numerous spanners and screwdrivers our new acquisition was assembled, fuelled, and ready to go! I turned the key and, to my joy, the engine burst into life and soon settled down to steady tick-over. I gave myself a pat on the back and then decided to test the generating side of the unit; it was then that I discovered the one subtle difference between my old 'genny' and its replacement. The outlet socket is 32 amp on the brand spanking new one, whereas all my leads and adaptors are 16amp (which fitted the old one) and, not wishing to bamboozle any of you with science, this simply means that, in order to suck 'juice' from this contraption I was in need of a much bigger plug than any that I had!

Now, late on a Sunday evening in the middle of a New Forest Inclosure is not the ideal time or place to locate a product that you wouldn't, ordinarily, expect to find on the shelves of B&Q or Homebase! I made several, futile calls to friends 'in the trade' and we finally went to bed, safe in the knowledge that in the workshop stood a gleaming generator with, unfortunately, no way of connecting it to the house!

And, of course, the inevitable happened. During the night a thumping great beech tree fell across our overhead supply wires and we awoke on Monday morning without power. A short trip to the wholesalers to

Replacement 'Genny'

acquire the necessary plug followed by a bit of twiddling with a screw driver quickly rectified the situation. The SEB engineer was soon with us to inspect the damage and make an assessment of the necessary remedial works; he assured us that a Lineman would be with us as soon as possible and that if I could clear the fallen tree it would help their overstretched resources. So out came the chainsaw and three hours later the cables, albeit it still dead on the ground, were free of obstruction!
In the event it wasn't until about 6.00pm on the following day that a two-man crew arrived and, bless them, they worked into the night in order to restore our electricity supply. When I queried the reason for the delay I was informed that as the damage only affected a single property, the repair was not a priority; and I reckon that's fair enough and all part of living here, but thank goodness something prompted me to go and buy that generator!!

Wishing you all a happy Christmas

The other books From a New Forest Inclosure

From A New Forest Inclosure
The First Two Years
Ian Thew

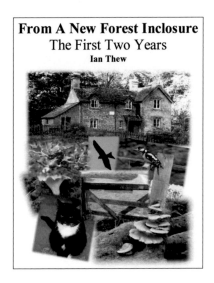

From a New Forest Inclosure
Book Two 2006 & 2007
Ian Tew

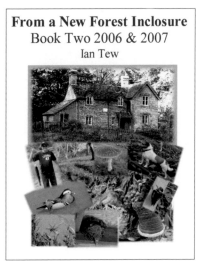

From a New Forest Inclosure
Book Three 2008 & 2009
Ian Thew

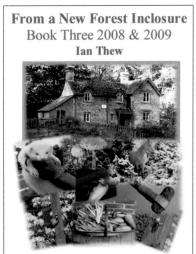

From A New Forest Inclosure
Book Four 2010 & 2011
Ian Thew

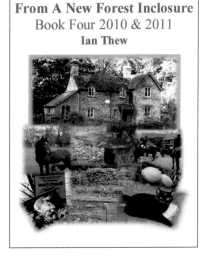

These books are available by post: Please send £5,99 per book plus £2.50 postage and packaging (up to five books) to Ian Thew, Burley Rails Cottage, Burley BH24 4HT England Or telephone 01425 403735 with your name, postal address Email ian@burleyrails.co.uk for BACS details.

Burley Rails Cottage, Wilfs Cabin and Paddocks

Wilfs Cabin

Stables

Wilfs Cabin; a self-contained, snug, traditional log cabin that provides a double bed room with en-suite shower, a cosy lounge and a galley kitchen. The timbered veranda is ideal for alfresco dining or for just relaxing with a glass of wine after a busy day in the Forest.

For the four legged visitors there are two, modern, block-built, stables with individual yards and a tack room with all facilities, which are adjacent to two small turn-out paddocks. There is ample parking and undercover storage for traps and bikes.

www.burleyrailscottage.co.uk   Tel:01425 403735

Well behaved and sociable dogs are also welcome.

NEWFOREST
Shooting & Fishing | Coaching & Tuition

The New Forest Fly Fishing and Shooting School was founded by Ian Thew who lives deep in the heart of the New Forest which is situated on the South Coast between the mighty rivers Test and Avon and offers the ultimate in fishing and shooting possibilities.

Our objective is to provide the very best in fly fishing and clay and game shooting for both the complete novice or the experienced sportsman and to this end we extend the opportunity to learn new skills or to hone existing expertise over a wide range of disciplines.

We take pride in providing instruction and coaching in all aspects of fishing and shooting to the very highest of standards and we take care to ensure that when our pupils leave us they will have been well versed in both safety and etiquette and will thus be able to move on in their selected sport with personal assurance and confidence.

Ian Thew is a qualified fly fishing coach and a qualified shooting instructor and, in addition to running the New Forest Fly Fishing and Shooting School, he writes regular features on all aspects of shooting, fishing and country sports related topics for magazines such as the Shooting Times and the Countrymans' weekly.

Ian is also a qualified deer stalker and over the past forty years he has amassed a unique and widespread knowledge of most rural activities from fishing to ferreting and just about everything else in between.

Contact Ian on 01425 403735 or email ian@ithew.freeserve.co.uk

www.shootingandfishingcoaching.co.uk